MILITARY SHIPS

AMPHIBIOUS ASSAULT SHIPS

BY JOHN HAMILTON

VISIT US AT
WWW.ABDOPUBLISHING.COM

Published by ABDO Publishing Company, PO Box 398166, Minneapolis, MN 55439.
Copyright ©2013 by Abdo Consulting Group, Inc. International copyrights reserved in all
countries. No part of this book may be reproduced in any form without written permission
from the publisher. A&D Xtreme™ is a trademark and logo of ABDO Publishing Company.

Printed in the United States of America, North Mankato, Minnesota.
032012
092012

Editor: Sue Hamilton
Graphic Design: Sue Hamilton
Cover Design: John Hamilton
Cover Photo: United States Navy
Interior Photos: All photos United States Navy except Getty Images-pg 8 and Northrop
Grumman Corporation-pgs 28-29.

ABDO Booklinks
Web sites about Military Ships are featured on our Book Links pages. These links are
routinely monitored and updated to provide the most current information available.
Web site: www.abdopublishing.com

Library of Congress Cataloging-in-Publication Data

Hamilton, John, 1959-
Amphibious assault ships / John Hamilton.
    p. cm. – (Military ships)
Includes index.
Audience: Age 8-15.
ISBN 978-1-61783-520-9
1. Amphibious assault ships- Juvenile literature. I. Title.
V895.H36 2012
623.825- dc23
                          2012005058

TABLE OF CONTENTS

AMPHIBIOUS ASSAULT SHIPS

Amphibious assault ships resemble small aircraft carriers. They have flat flight decks. They also have tower-like structures called islands. But these ships carry mostly helicopters and smaller boats. They support United States Marines who attack enemy shores.

Amphibious assault ships are often nicknamed "gator ships," or "gator freighters."

MISSIONS

Amphibious assault ships bring United States Marines, their weapons, supplies, and heavy vehicles to enemy beaches.

A Sea Knight helicopter hovers as Marines position themselves on the flight deck of the USS Makin Island.

XTREME FACT

Amphibious assault ships are often named after World War II aircraft carriers, or other famous U.S. Navy ships.

Their flight decks are used to launch helicopters, rotary winged aircraft, and jets that can take off vertically. These aircraft support the Marines as they fight the enemy.

HISTORY

During World War II (1939-1945), United States Marines assaulted beaches controlled by Japan and Germany. Small escort carriers launched planes to support the Marines.

Marines storm the shores of the island of Guadalcanal in August 1942. This was the first major U.S. and Allied forces strike against Japan during World War II.

Military helicopters were developed and improved in the 1950s and 1960s. Marines and their equipment could be transported by helicopter or small landing craft on coasts almost anywhere in the world.

XTREME FACT

U.S. Navy Tarawa-class amphibious assault ships entered service in the late 1970s. The USS Peleliu is still in service today (as of 2012).

A Sea Cobra helicopter armed with Sidewinder missiles sits on the deck of the USS Tarawa in 1989.

WASP-CLASS SHIPS

Wasp-class ships were first built in the 1980s. They replace older Tarawa-class ships.

A Harrier jet lands aboard the USS Essex.

Wasp-class ships were built to use Harrier jets and LCAC landing craft. These ships also sometimes use the new V-22 Osprey tilt-rotor aircraft.

AMPHIBIOUS ASSAULT SHIPS FAST FACTS

Wasp-Class Specifications

Length:	844 feet (257 m)
Width (beam):	106 feet (32 m)
Displacement (loaded):	45,528 tons (41,302 metric tons)
Propulsion:	Two boilers, two propeller shafts
Speed:	20-plus knots (23 mph/37 kph)
Crew:	66 — Officers
	1,004 — Sailors
	1,871 — Marines
Aircraft:	Mix of Sea Stallion helicopters, Sea Knight helicopters, Harrier jets, Huey helicopters, Super Cobra helicopters, Osprey tilt-rotor aircraft.

The USS Boxer *is one of eight Wasp-class amphibious assault ships in the United States Navy.*

CONSTRUCTION

The USS Makin Island under construction in Pascagoula, MS, in 2006.

Navy amphibious assault ships are built by Huntington Ingalls Industries. The shipyard is in Pascagoula, Mississippi. The vessels are assembled in large sections. They are then welded together. Ships are launched into the water when they are nearly complete. Soon, the ships are ready for testing. This is called a sea trial.

XTREME FACT

The USS Wasp was built with 21,000 tons (19,051 metric tons) of steel and 400 tons (363 metric tons) of aluminum. Each of its two propellers is 16 feet (5 m) in diameter.

The huge propellers of the amphibious assault ship USS Bonhomme Richard are displayed while repairs are made on the ship.

CREW

Wasp-class ships include a crew of 1,004 enlisted sailors. They are commanded by 66 officers. There are many jobs, from cooks to pilots. These ships are like floating bases for U.S. Marines. Up to 1,871 Marines can be transported by a single ship.

XTREME FACT

Amphibious assault ships also carry special forces troops, such as Navy SEALs.

Crew members steer the
USS Kearsarge from the
ship's bridge.

FLIGHT DECK

The flight deck is the flat area where aircraft take off and land. Wasp-class ships have nine landing spots for helicopters. CH-46 Sea Knight helicopters carry troops and cargo. AH-1J Sea Cobra attack helicopters help Marines when they invade enemy beaches.

An Osprey is guided to a landing on the flight deck of the USS Makin Island.

Older helicopters are being replaced by V-22 Osprey tilt-rotor aircraft. They land and takeoff like helicopters, but fly like turboprop aircraft.

A Harrier jet makes a vertical landing on the deck of the USS Peleliu.

The AV-8B Harrier II ground-attack jet can take off and land vertically on the ship's short flight deck. Each ship normally carries six Harriers.

THE ISLAND

The island is the large, tower-like structure that sits on the top deck. The island is several stories tall. It has radar and communications antennas to keep track of nearby ships and planes.

The island of the USS Essex.

Sailors on the bridge of the USS Essex control the ship.

The ship's captain and other officers control the vessel from the bridge.

THE HANGAR

Two large elevators move helicopters, jets, and heavy equipment from the flight deck to storage in the ship's cavernous hangar bay within the hull. Each elevator can lift up to 75,000 pounds (34,019 kg). Other equipment is moved by six cargo elevators and a high-speed monorail system.

An Osprey sits in the hangar bay of the USS Iwo Jima.

5849
E M
04
MARINE
VMM-261

XTREME FACT

A Wasp-class amphibious assault ship has about 100,000 cubic feet (2,832 cubic meters) of additional cargo holds throughout the vessel.

WELL DECK

A well deck is a deck on the bottom of a ship's stern, or back. It can be flooded and opened so that smaller boats can dock safely inside the ship.

An assault craft unit enters the well deck of the USS Essex.

1631

1631

1631

Most Wasp-class amphibious assault ships have well decks that are 267 feet (81 m) long, 50 feet (15 m) wide, with an area of 13,000 square feet (1,208 square meters).

XTREME FACT

During a beach assault, well decks can ballast over 15,000 tons (13,608 metric tons) of seawater when launching amphibious landing craft.

LANDING CRAFT

The Navy's LCAC is a large transport craft. It shuttles Marines and heavy equipment to enemy shores. It rides on a cushion of air. LCACs have a range of 200 miles (322 km).

An LCAC launches from the well deck of the amphibious assault ship USS Wasp.

LCACs can move faster than 40 knots (46 mph/74 kph). They can carry more than 60 tons (54 metric tons) of equipment, including tanks and artillery.

XTREME FACT

LCAC stands for "Landing Craft, Air Cushion."

AMERICA-CLASS SHIPS

The USS *America* is the newest version of the U.S. Navy's amphibious assault ship fleet. It is scheduled to be completed in 2014.

An artist's drawing of the USS America.

America-class ships are built to carry advanced F-35 Lightning II aircraft and Osprey tilt-rotor aircraft. The ships' two propellers will be driven by either gas turbines or electric engines.

GLOSSARY

ALLIES
The Allies were the many nations that were allied, or joined, in the fight against Germany, Italy, and Japan in World War II. The most powerful nations among the Allies included the United States, Great Britain, the Soviet Union, France, China, Canada, and Australia.

ARTILLERY
Large weapons of war, such as cannons, howitzers, and missile launchers, used by military forces on land.

BOILER
A container that is capable of generating steam by applying heat. On Navy ships, boilers generate the steam that powers the ship.

DISPLACEMENT
Displacement is a way of measuring a ship's mass, or size. It equals the weight of the water a ship displaces, or occupies, while floating. Think of a bathtub filled to the rim with water. A toy boat placed in the tub would cause water to spill over the sides. The weight of that water equals the weight of the boat.

ENLISTED
A military service person who joined the armed forces, but is not an officer.

Hull
The hull is the main body of a ship, including the bottom, sides, and deck.

LCAC
An abbreviation for "Landing Craft, Air Cushion." A ship also known as a hovercraft that moves on a cushion of air above the water or ground.

Radar
A way to detect objects, such as aircraft or ships, using electromagnetic (radio) waves. Radar waves are sent out by large dishes, or antennas, and then strike an object. The radar dish then detects the reflected wave, which can tell operators how big an object is, how fast it is moving, its altitude, and its direction.

Sea Trial
The first test cruise of a newly constructed ship. It is the last step in construction. Also called a "shakedown cruise," this first trip at sea may last from a few hours to several days. The ship's speed, maneuverability, equipment, and safety features are tested.

Tilt-Rotor
An aircraft, such as the V-22 Osprey, that has movable rotors at the end of each wing, allowing it to take off and land vertically, as well as fly forward and backward.

INDEX